A New Kind of Leader

A NEW KIND OF LEADER
Published by Orange
a division of The reThink Group, Inc.
5870 Charlotte Lane, Suite 300
Cumming, GA 30040 U.S.A.

The Orange logo is a registered trademark of The reThink Group, Inc.

Other Orange products are available online and direct from the publisher. Volume discounts are available for churches and other organizations. Visit our website at www.ThinkOrange.com.

978-1-941259072-6

©2016 Reggie Joiner

Editing Team: Kristen Ivy & Mike Jeffries
Art Direction: Ryan Boon
Illustrations: The Sketch Effect
Layout and Design: FiveStone

Printed in the United States of America
First Edition 2016

3 4 5 6 7 8 9 10 11 12

01/20/17

REGGIE JOINER

A New Kind of Leader

WHAT YOU BELIEVE CAN OPEN A DOOR FOR A KID OR TEENAGER'S FUTURE

TABLE OF CONTENTS

WE STARTED ORANGE SEVERAL YEARS AGO TO "INFLUENCE THOSE WHO INFLUENCE THE NEXT GENERATION."

OUR PREMISE IS SIMPLE.

If you combine the heart of the family (red)
with the light of the church (yellow),
you will make a greater impact.

Heart of Family + Light of Church = Orange

This idea is built on the notion that . . .
Two combined influences will make a greater impact than just two influences.

This mindset is championed by an innovative, passionate group of leaders who come from various styles and sizes of churches. These leaders are collectively beginning a revolution as thought leaders and pioneers who are determined to build authentic faith in the next generation.

This book is a concise guide to some of the **common values** that connect these individuals we see as a **new kind of leader**.

WIDE OPEN

In Bethel Church, outside of Wrightsville, Georgia, there hangs an oil painting of Jesus knocking on a door.

The painting is the artwork of Geneva Delphia Bray, who was born in 1883, on a farm about a mile down a country dirt road from Bethel Church.

There was nothing exceptionally noteworthy about Geneva's life; except that she lived through . . .
two world wars,
the Great Depression,
women's suffrage,
the Civil Rights Movement,
the Vietnam War,
the invention of Apple computers,
and 23 of our nation's presidents.

Most people who knew Geneva knew . . .
she lived in the white farmhouse on Bill Oliver Road.
she spent most of her life without indoor plumbing.
she once tied a duck to a table so she could paint its picture.

Only a few people who knew Geneva knew...

she never married because of a broken heart.
she was forced to quit her education because her dad decided it was a waste of money to send a girl to college.
she never drove a car—however, in her fifties, she did hitch a ride every weekend to finish that college degree.

Probably the most remarkable thing about Geneva was that she taught elementary school for forty years. It's hard to tell how many children she influenced—but I know of one.

She was a nine-year-old girl who almost became an orphan. The girl's birth mother gave her up for adoption shortly after she was born. Then her adoptive parents each committed suicide one year apart. Alone at nine years old, no one wanted to assume responsibility for her. Until Geneva said, "Well, no one has asked me if I would take her!"

So at 54 years of age, Geneva opened her door and raised the little girl as her own. That girl was my mom. And from that day when my mom walked through the door of that old farmhouse, Geneva became known to our family as Aunt Nennie.

It's sobering to think about the difference one person can make in someone else's future.

Of course, there were others who impacted my mom through the years. Like most of us, a number of people influenced her life by showing up at just the right time. But there is no doubt that one person radically changed the direction of my mom's story.

More than likely, Aunt Nennie never fully realized the kind of impact she made in Mom's life and the lives of our entire family. When you invest in someone else, you seldom see immediate results. You typically don't realize in the present how you are affecting someone else's future.

I'm sure Aunt Nennie had no idea when she opened her door, built an extra bedroom onto the farmhouse, cooked a country diet of fried chicken and creamed corn, made Mom attend Bethel Church every week, pushed Mom to make good grades, intimidated all of Mom's potential boyfriends, helped Mom get into college, paid for Mom's wedding, and loved Mom unconditionally, that it would have a ripple effect on the faith of generations.

As a kid, I used to sit in Bethel Church on Sundays and stare at Aunt Nennie's picture of Jesus.

It helped distract me from the hard pews and the long sermons, not to mention the Georgia summer heat.

I remember asking her one day, "So whose house is Jesus knocking on?" She explained, "It's not really a house. It's the door to your heart. That's why Jesus said, 'I stand at the door and knock; if anyone hears my voice and opens the door, I will come in and eat with that person and they with me.'" Then, after looking at the picture closely, I told her it didn't seem like she had finished painting it. "Why do you think that?," she asked. And I answered, "Because you didn't put a handle on the door."

Aunt Nennie smiled and explained, "Oh, I did that on purpose. The door can only be opened from the inside. That's because Jesus never forces his way into anyone's life. You have to invite Him in. Once you do, He invites you into a different kind of life."

I wish I could have heard Aunt Nennie explain that picture to my mom as a nine-year-old girl. Mom had known enough pain, unpredictability, and rejection that I'm sure she was ready to be invited into a different kind of life.

I imagine as soon as she heard that Jesus was knocking, she swung the door to her heart open pretty fast. And I'm positively sure that once she opened the door to her heart, she forgot to close it back. She just left it wide open for anyone else to come in too.

This was also true in a literal sense. When we were growing up, the door to our house stayed unlocked and everyone knew they didn't have to knock before coming inside.

The problem is that sometimes Mom assumed that everyone else should leave their doors open too. She had a tendency to invite herself into everyone's lives without knocking— every waitress, every stranger, every relative, everyone else's relative, every co-worker, every pastor, and even her daughter-in-laws.

Yes, there were times when she got carried away. And no, sometimes she did not understand healthy boundaries. But I'm glad she chose to live life with an open door instead of the alternative. Mom simply made the assumption that when you welcome Jesus into your house or heart, then you have to welcome everyone else the way Jesus would. That's just how it works. You simply can't close the door behind Jesus if you really understand the Gospel.

I hate to admit it, but sometimes I look at a child's situation and wonder, "Will believing in Jesus really make a difference in this kid's life?"

Then I think about my mom.

And I am reminded of what can happen to the future of any child or teenager who welcomes Jesus into their life. I am more convinced than ever that leading kids into a relationship with Jesus is worth it.

There will probably be times when you wonder if what you are doing for a kid really matters. You may even question, "Am I good enough, smart enough, or even qualified enough to help a child?"

The more important question is: "Do you care enough?" Opening your door to a child doesn't mean you have to let someone move into your house, but it does imply that you are willing to assume a role in shaping a child's faith.

If I could introduce you to Aunt Nennie, I know she would tell you it's worth it to show up for a child. I also think she would probably say, "When Jesus knocks on your door, expect there to be some kids behind Him waiting to come in."

This book is built on the assumption that:
Somewhere along your path,
an adult opened the door for you.

If you're reading this, it could be because someone is trying to manipulate you into caring about kids the same way someone cared about you.

That's okay.

If you had . . .
a mother who gave birth to you,
a guardian who didn't let you starve to death,
a teacher who kept pushing you to learn something,
or any adult who kept you from running into the middle of a busy street,
then you should be willing to give a little of your time to a kid.

Think about it this way:
If you presently exist, it's only because someone, somewhere, cared enough to be present in your life.

It's easy to forget that it took a few caring adults to help you make it through your childhood.

And if someone gave you enough time and attention to help
you get where you are, then you should probably do the same
for some
sweaty
sticky
smelly
snotty
snobby
selfish
stubborn
CHILD who acts like you did when you were that age.

Most of you have a short list of names of people who
impacted your childhood and teenage years. When those
individuals intersected with your world, they became a new
kind of leader.

They were not *new* in the sense that
they had never led anything before or
they were radically different than other leaders.

But they were new because . . .
their influence gave you a new direction.
their belief in you gave you a new sense of worth.
they showed up at a new phase of your life,
and in some new way helped shape your future.

There are pivotal moments in every kid's life when they need a new kind of leader who will show them something new about God or life.

Someone did that for you and the challenging question this book asks is, "How will you do it for someone else?"

If you are presently making an investment in a child or teenager, it's probably *not* because you are . . .
a skilled communicator,
a celebrity who raised millions for a cause,
or a professional expert who advocates for kids.

You do it simply because you love a child or teenager and care about their future faith.

The fact that you are reading this book suggests there is a spark of interest and concern for some kid's future. That's all it takes to get started. So get ready. If this book came with a warning label, it would say, "Opening your door to kids will change you more than it changes them."

We hope these pages will help you reimagine how you can love and lead the next generation. There are kids everywhere that need a new kind of leader.

1

THERE'S A NEW KIND OF
LEADER WHO BELIEVES

KIDS
MATTER

MORE THAN ADULTS

MAYBE YOU'RE THINKING THAT THE STATEMENT, "KIDS MATTER MORE THAN ADULTS," IS A LITTLE EXTREME. IF YOU'RE AN ADULT, YOU MIGHT BE EVEN SLIGHTLY OFFENDED.

Before you discredit the idea as too radical, think about it. Even your dog figures this out pretty quickly. When a new baby arrives, everyone's status changes.

I'm not trying to devalue any human at any stage of life. The statement isn't intended to imply that an adult's life has any less value than a kid's life, nor that the world should in any way revolve around a child. What it does suggest is that if you want to affect the way a generation sees the world, then it makes sense to start influencing their character and faith when they are young.

Every expert agrees that the first eighteen years of a person's life are extremely crucial in laying a foundation for their future. But the tension is that even though a lot of people might agree that kids matter, sometimes we fail to act like it. What if there really was a new kind of leader who believed that every phase of a kid's life—from birth through adolescence—really matters?

What if you started acting like
**WHAT YOU DO FOR KIDS IS MORE IMPORTANT
THAN ANYTHING ELSE YOU DO.**

By *kids*, we mean anyone who is not yet an adult.
And no, that does not include Uncle Frank and his fourth-
grade sense of humor. We are thinking of anyone between the
ages of zero and around twenty.

It may not seem like what you do for kids is all that significant.
Sometimes it's just . . .
showing up to change a diaper.
remembering the name of a pet goldfish.
filling endless quantities of water balloons.
writing a text to say you're praying for their test.

Even when it seems insignificant, what you do for a kid early
on will leave an impression. And early impressions matter
more than we think.

Sue Gerhardt, a researcher on emotional health in children,
says a child's brain "is built up through actual experiences.
What you put in is more or less what you get out."[1]

---

1 – Sue Gerhart, *Why Love Matters: How Affection Shapes a Baby's Brain* (New York:
Routledge, 2005), 89

That's why what you do for a kid is like making an investment. It gains more value over time.

The sooner you start paying in, the greater the return will be later. The longer you wait, the less you earn.

Simply put:
Making deposits in someone's life while they are young will earn more interest.

When you wait until they're adults, the gains are slower.

We could restate the original principle this way:
What you do now for a kid is more important than what you do for them later as an adult.

Our team is leading an in-depth research project called "It's Just a Phase." Our goal is to interview reputable educators, counselors, and pediatricians, and to review the best books ever written on the topic of child development. What we are discovering both confirms and challenges much of what we believe about shaping the faith and character of kids. These discoveries are also launching a new initiative in our organization to influence parents and leaders to rethink how they love and lead kids.[2]

---

2 Follow along with this initiative at www.justaphase.com

Imagine if you waited until a child became an adult before you taught him or her to read. Parents who want their child to become educated adults enroll their child in school. They pack a backpack for today, so their child is educated for the future.

No wonder *adult* governments pass common-sense laws to ensure the educational and physical well-being of the average child. Why? Because what happens to kids matters more.

According to the World Health Organization, "The early years of life are crucial in influencing a range of health and social outcomes across the lifecourse. Research now shows that many challenges in adult society—mental health problems, obesity, stunting, criminality, heart disease, competence in literacy and numeracy—have their roots in early childhood."[3]

So if it's important to start guarding the mental and physical health of a kid's life now, then what about their moral, emotional, relational, and spiritual growth? It's naïve to think that what happens in a kid's life now really doesn't matter as much as what happens to them later. It's not a leap to suggest that what happens now in their life relationally and spiritually will also impact their future in exponential ways. The early years shape so much of an individual's sense of purpose, belonging, and identity.

3 - Lori G. Irwin Arjumand Siddiqi Clyde Hertzman, *Early Child Development: A Powerful Equalizer*, Final Report for the World Health Organization's Commission on the Social Determinants of Health, June 2007, 4

Here's another thought:
what your church does for kids is more important than anything else your church does.

I know what you're thinking.
Preschoolers take up a lot of room.
Children can't sit sill.
Teenagers don't dress appropriately.
But what you do for kids matters both for kids and for your church.

What you do for kids will transform the culture of your church.
Something transformational happens in churches when more children and teenagers are around.
Parents become more engaged.
Volunteers become more motivated.
Staffs become more focused.
Everybody becomes more involved.
Your church will love deeper, think harder, laugh louder, and pray more. I might even make the argument that your pastor's sermons could become more interesting. (But I don't want to overpromise.) I do believe a few more kids can change the dynamic and the energy of your entire church.

*What you do for kids will keep your
church from dying.*

The age of the average church member increases by seven
years every decade and in the next ten years, the average
age of members in many mainline denominations will be
over sixty. In most places, the average age of a churchgoer is
fifteen years older than the surrounding community members.
Basically, churches are "greying" because members are
getting older, and younger families are just not attending. The
only way to reverse the trend is to reach more kids.

That's one reason you might consider opening the door a little
wider for kids in your community—just to make sure that the
doors of your church are never permanently closed.

That's what Dalton Baptist Church, a congregation near
Scranton, Pennsylvania, did. There were barely a dozen
senior adults left attending the church so they voted to do
something unusual. Instead of letting their church age out
of existence, they donated their building to a youth ministry
from a church up the street. When asked why they did it, one
of the elders replied, "We believe it's our mission to keep the
doors open."

Maybe you should take your cue from Jesus.
Think about how Jesus challenged His culture to shift the way they thought about children.

Jesus evidently had a pretty high opinion of kids.
Remember, He actually said, *"Whoever welcomes one such child in my name welcomes me."*

In other words, He said, "I want you to treat kids like you would treat me. And by the way, just in case you haven't figured it out by now, I am God. So just make sure you understand that when you welcome kids, it's like you are welcoming God."

Okay, that's a paraphrase, but you have to admit,
Jesus made every kid a pretty big deal.

It was like Jesus was suggesting . . .
no one should feel more welcome at your church than a screaming baby.
no one should feel more welcome at your church than a bratty kid.
no one should feel more welcome at your church than a hormonal middle schooler.
no one should feel more welcome at your church than a defiant teenager.

So what if kids don't . . .
sound like God.
act like God.
smell like God.

You should welcome every kid and every teenager as if you were welcoming God. And if there's one thing Jesus modeled for us clearly, it was that the people who follow Him should welcome kids.

Jesus positioned Himself as the way to know God, then He threw the door wide open.

That's why the Pharisees panicked. They had an identity crisis because there were people walking through the door who didn't look like they did.

If everyone in your church is comfortable with who is showing up on Sundays, then you haven't opened the door wide enough.

You can almost hear Jesus saying, "See those tax collectors, let them in!" "See those prostitutes, let them in!" "See that Samaritan woman, let her in!" "See those middle schoolers, let them in!"

That's why He's expecting you to keep the door open.

KIDS NEED A NEW KIND OF LEADER WHO WILL
VOLUNTEER TO DO SOMETHING MORE.

///

Maybe you should just simply decide:
You will do what someone did for you.
You will do what you wish someone had done for you.
You will do what you hope someone will do
for your kid or grandkid one day.

Let's pretend I was your pastor (now, that's a scary thought).
But if I were, here's what I might say:

"No one can volunteer for anything until we have enough
leaders for kids and teenagers."

"We are canceling Sunday morning adult classes,
so you no longer have an excuse."

"If you haven't volunteered for over two years,
you need to go to another church."

Okay, maybe I shouldn't have to say any of those things and you should just do one of the following:

If you are not volunteering, start. *Don't wait to be asked. Take the initiative.*

If you are volunteering some, consider volunteering more. *Getting more involved will change you more than them.*

If you are volunteering a lot, go find someone else to volunteer with you. *The best new volunteers are usually recruited by the best already-existing volunteers.*

KIDS
MATTER

MORE THAN ADULTS

WHAT IF YOU STARTED ACTING LIKE

WHAT YOU DO FOR KIDS IS MORE IMPORTANT THAN ANYTHING ELSE YOU DO

KIDS NEED
A NEW KIND
OF LEADER
WHO WILL

VOLUNTEER TO DO SOMETHING MORE

MAKE A LIST HERE OF TWO OR THREE PEOPLE WHO INSPIRED
YOU WHEN YOU WERE A CHILD OR TEENAGER.
DESCRIBE HOW THEY MADE YOU FEEL.
LIST A FEW OF THEIR QUALITIES.

MAKE A LIST OF PEOPLE YOU KNOW YOU COULD
RECOMMEND AS VOLUNTEERS.

....

....

....

....

....

....

....

....

....

....

....

....

2

THERE'S A NEW KIND OF
LEADER WHO BELIEVES

A STRATEGY
MATTERS

MORE THAN YOU THINK

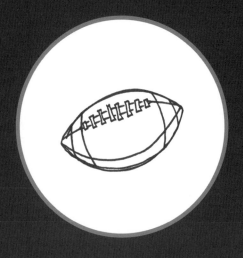

HERE'S A WARNING:
IF YOU ARE A LEADER WHO BELIEVES THAT KIDS MATTER, AT SOME POINT YOU WILL TRY TO CHANGE SOME THINGS.

Why? Because you realize that what's happening in a kid's world now will shape their world as an adult.

But before you . . .
order orange paint for every room,
build a treehouse inside the sanctuary,
move your flat screen TV to the church,
install a rock wall for middle schoolers,
give the teenagers the key to your house,
or convince the elders to hand over the worship budget,
take a minute to ask yourself a few questions.

What do you want kids to grow up and believe?
What exactly is your responsibility as a volunteer?
What are you hoping to convince parents to do?
What will be the best way to measure success?

In other words . . .
What is your strategy?

We define strategy as *a plan of action with an end in mind.* So when I ask, "What is your strategy?" I am really asking you to clarify two things:

What do you want to accomplish in a kid's life?
What are the action steps that will help you make
that happen?

Here's another way to think about it.
Your strategy has the potential to connect your
leaders,
resources,
events,
and curriculum
into one integrated plan to lead a child or teenager into a growing relationship with Jesus.

A strategy links whatever you have to wherever you are going. Without a strategy, all of your assets lose their potential to have collective influence. They are kind of like individual football players who all play independently.

Can you imagine saying to a college football coach, "Don't worry about a strategy. Just send your best 11 players out on the field, give them the ball and tell them to score." It would be a sad game.

Even if every player trained on the best exercise equipment, played in a state-of-the-art stadium, and dressed in the most expensive gear, the team wouldn't move the ball very far. The odds would be stacked against them if they didn't have a strategy.

Having a strategy matters more than you think.
You might even say your strategy matters more than your mission. I'm not suggesting your mission isn't important. I'm just saying that . . .

**It's your strategy, not your mission,
that determines your success.**

A lot of churches and organizations with great missions have ceased to exist. The reason they failed in their mission was not because they didn't believe what is true, have good ideas or recruit incredible people. It was because they couldn't develop and execute an effective strategy.

It's easy to skip over the issue of strategy. We meet churches all the time that have good motives and great leaders but just can't seem to get momentum. Why? Because *good intentions without an intentional strategy won't lead anyone very far.*

What if you started acting like
**YOU AREN'T REALLY LEADING KIDS ANYWHERE
IF YOU DON'T HAVE A PLAN.**

Think about the orange traffic cones used to direct cars at a big concert or event. Imagine what would happen if someone just scattered the cones randomly across the parking lot. More than likely, it would create a traffic jam and cars would not be able to move anywhere.

But when the cones are arranged strategically, they have the potential to move hundreds of vehicles exactly where they need to go.

Now imagine that your church's weekly programs, annual events, kid's groups, and age-specific curriculums are like traffic cones. How you arrange them to work together is important. They are either strategic or random.

Here's a question you should ask about the ministry where you serve: Is what we do with children and teenagers characterized by random activities or by strategic steps that lead Kids somewhere.

Being strategic doesn't mean you shouldn't be flexible.
A good leader will know how to adjust when . . .
it's worship time, but a toddler does the potty dance.
the activity calls for dried peas, and you have M&Ms.
a teenager texts on Monday to say she's failing math.

But being strategic does imply that all of your activities
and resources are aligned around a clear plan so they work
together to lead a kid where you want them to go.

If you don't have a plan, then maybe you aren't really leading
kids anywhere.

One of the things our "Just a Phase" research has confirmed
is the importance of a strategic leader being present at every
phase of a kid's life.

Kids navigate unique challenges at each phase. So they
need a new kind of leader who will show up to keep them
from getting stuck.

Kids face critical transitions as they move from phase to phase.
That's why they need a new kind of leader who will stand in
the gap, and help them keep moving in the right direction.
Remember, you are that leader.

Since strategy involves having a plan of action with an end in mind, it's important for you to answer at least two questions about the kids you lead.

 What do you want kids to become?

When kids grow up and leave your church, what do you want their faith and character to look like? You can ask the same question a few different ways.

During their freshman or sophomore year of college, when they are sitting in their dorm rooms, what do you want them to remember?

When they get their first job or rent an apartment, how do you want them to relate to God, the world, and themselves as a result of being in your church?

When every leader and parent can agree on a clear and concise answer to those questions, it will give you a common language. Speaking the same language has a way of keeping everyone focused on what matters most. And speaking the same language makes it easier for everyone to lead kids in the same direction.

We believe Jesus gave us the answer to the question: What do you want a kid to become?

It happened when a religious leader asked, *"Teacher, which is the greatest commandment in the law?"*

Jesus' response was timeless: *"Love the Lord your God with all your heart and with all your soul and with all your mind. This is the first and greatest commandment. And the second is like it: Love your neighbor as yourself. All the Law and the Prophets hang on these two commandments." (Matthew 22:36-37).*

There is a lot packed into His response. Jesus hung everything that matters on one big idea: LOVE. He clarified that the main priority is a relationship that starts with God.

So what if everything you do simply leads kids to
Love God
Love Others
Love Life

That means whatever you do or say should help move kids to become people who love God in a way that affects the rest of their world.

The second strategic question is . . .

 2 **Where do you want kids to be?**

The first question, "What do you want kids to become?" implies you're leading them in a direction.

The second question, "Where do you want kids to be?" suggests you're leading them to a destination.

Both questions actually point to relationships. Again, maybe it will help give clarity if I ask the second question in a few different ways. See if these make sense . . .

What is the optimal environment in your church where kids can grow in their relationship with Jesus?

If every week in your church, children or teenagers could only go to one place,
experience one environment,
or participate in one activity,
what would you tell them to do?

Once you decide the answer, everything else you do should work as a strategic step to that environment.

The way you answer this question matters because your church has limited . . .
resources,
volunteers,
and time.
So it's important for you to know how to prioritize which environment in your church is most important.

Again, it's difficult to lead kids somewhere if you don't know where you are leading them.

So what is your answer to the question:
Where do you want kids to be?
Is it Sunday school?
Is it a student gathering?

Wherever it is, you need to know the answer. Until you do, you can't be strategic in how you lead kids.

We think the best answer to the question is *whichever environment connects a small group of kids with a consistent leader.* We call that a small group.

You can pick a different answer, but just remember that everything else you do will be affected by how you respond to these two strategic questions.

Having a plan with a clear end in mind means your
weekly curriculum,
seasonal events,
and primary influencers
should all work together to lead kids (at every phase) to love
Jesus, love others, and love life.

We think that happens best when every resource and leader
works as a step to build community in a small group context.

No one illustrates the value of strategy more than Nehemiah.
The walls of Jerusalem had been broken down for 150 years,
but before Nehemiah rallied other leaders and acquired
resources, he rode around the walls to devise a plan. Then
Nehemiah created a team of leaders and families who could
carry out that plan.

Strategy gives you a team advantage. Like Nehemiah, a new
kind of leader can change the future of the next generation if
they stay focused and passionate, and if they combine what
they do with what others do.

KIDS NEED A NEW KIND OF LEADER WHO WILL
PLAY AS A TEAM.

//

Leaders who play as a team will . . .

ARTICULATE THE COMMON LANGUAGE
*by using terms in your church culture and age-specific
curriculums that will stick in the minds of kids.*

STAY FOCUSED ON WHAT MATTERS MOST
*by remembering that your priority is helping every kid become
someone who loves God, others, and life.*

MOVE KIDS TOWARD POSITIVE RELATIONSHIPS
*by using every weekly program and event to lead a kid toward
a consistent small group experience.*

CHAMPION WHATEVER NEEDS TO CHANGE
*by becoming an advocate with other leaders for the needs of
children and teenagers.*

FOLLOW THE LEADER
by supporting and encouraging whoever drives the strategy.

A STRATEGY MATTERS

MORE THAN YOU THINK

WHAT IF YOU STARTED ACTING LIKE

YOU AREN'T REALLY LEADING KIDS ANYWHERE IF YOU DON'T HAVE A PLAN

KIDS NEED
A NEW KIND
OF LEADER
WHO WILL

PLAY AS A TEAM

IDENTIFY WHAT YOU WANT KIDS TO BECOME AND WHERE
YOU WANT THEM TO BE. DOES YOUR STRATEGY LEAD THEM
THERE IN AN INTENTIONAL WAY?

3

THERE'S A NEW KIND OF
LEADER WHO BELIEVES

YOUR CHURCH
MATTERS

BECAUSE IT'S A PLACE

IF YOU'RE READING THIS, I HOPE YOU BELIEVE YOUR CHURCH MATTERS FOR A LOT OF REASONS.

You learned some great songs about your Ebenezer.
(Maybe you should Google that word.)

You always had something to do on the weekends.
(That was before you could binge-watch on Netflix.)

You got free grape juice or wine.
(. . . depending on your denomination.)

Maybe you even met your wife or husband there.
(The church predated Match.com by 2,000 years.)

Okay. Maybe there are better reasons why your church matters. But here is a sobering thought: You are surrounded by people in your community who don't think your church matters at all.

How do I know? Because nearly 75 percent of them don't go to church. Not because they are anti-your church, but because they are truly oblivious to your church's existence. They don't hate your church. They just don't think about your church.

Before we go any further, we need to address the elephant in this book.

This book is not just about you as a new kind of leader. It's also about your church.

Nothing you read in this book will be very helpful if you can't get someone to understand why your church matters. And before that can happen, you have to genuinely and passionately believe that your church matters.

Imagine you are at the grocery store or your favorite restaurant, and someone corners you and says, "So really, why *does* your church matter?" What would you say?

Have you seriously considered that question enough to have crafted an answer?

Here's an optional answer. It's not a complete answer, and it's not the only answer. But until you come up with a better answer, you can borrow this one:

"My church matters because it's a place where I can help other people and other people can help me win at what really matters."

There's a lot packed into that one sentence, but every word counts. So let's amplify it.

Your church is a *place* (a physical location)
where *you* (an individual)
can *help* (get involved using your gifts and talents)
other people (someone else besides you)
and *other people* (a community that loves you)
can *help* (use their gifts and talents)
you *win* (keep moving in the right direction)
at *what really matters* (God, Jesus, family, relationships, worth, life, purpose, worship, truth, belonging, identity, vocation, love, etc.).

Did you notice how the sentence starts? With the idea that your church is a place. Practically speaking, your church is a physical location where people actually gather and do something.

For nearly 2,000 years, churches have met in homes, catacombs, restaurants, cathedrals, tents, theaters, town halls, coffeehouses, storefronts, schools, and hotels. Regardless of creed or style, the local church has always been a place where people can actually sit down—to learn, worship, think, serve, celebrate, and sometimes even eat together.

I can hear an urgent, skeptical voice in my head saying, "But the church is *people*!" And theologically, that voice is exactly right. Jesus changed centuries of worship defined by a physical structure when He showed up on the planet. When He told Peter, "On this rock, I will build my church," He was not talking about constructing a new kind of edifice. The New Testament distinctly defines the church as a body of believers (people), not a building.

So let's assume we all understand that. Let's also acknowledge that your church meets in a place. This place isn't the church, but without the place, you wouldn't have a place to meet. I know you're glad I cleared that up—it was starting to get confusing.

Here's the point. It's important to think about church as a place simply because kids need a place. Before they can wrestle with abstract concepts like grace, hope, and forgiveness, kids need a place where they can connect with people who are the church.

A kid's faith can grow in relationships, but those relationships need a meeting place. Stated another way: If there is no place to connect, then chances are no one is actually connecting.

What if you started acting like
**YOU MAY BE THE BEST CHANCE A KID
WILL HAVE TO FIND A PLACE TO BELONG.**

People gravitate to where they feel accepted. Yet that desire for acceptance can make kids vulnerable to negative influences. If your church doesn't give kids a place to belong, you can bet somebody else will.

Never underestimate how much the right place can affect and enrich relationships. Think of some of the best friendships you know. There is probably a memorable gathering place that stands as an iconic symbol of the relationship.
Saved by the Bell had a diner.
Friends had a coffee shop.
Buffy had a dance club.
Cheers had a bar.

Okay. Those may not be the best examples of relationships. But they all speak to the power of having a place "where everybody knows your name." When you get serious about influencing the hearts of this generation, you start thinking about creating a visible, tangible place where kids know they belong.

That means you have to realize something important.
You can't make relationships happen.
You can only create environments
that make it easier for relationships to happen.

If I can oversimplify your role for kids, I would say your job is to create environments where kids can effectively connect with leaders and each other.

So if you want your church to matter to a kid, you have to care about the kind of specific place you are creating for a child or teenager. How you arrange, decorate, and organize your space will determine how kids connect—or disengage—with your church.

Think about it this way:
Your church can't make kids follow Jesus.
Your church can't insist that kids come every Sunday.
Your church can't force kids to build relationships.
But your church *can* create environments where kids actually want to be and where they know they belong.

What if every kid grew up in your church believing, "There's always a seat at the table for me"? Better yet, what if every kid or teenager who doesn't go to your church started believing they have a place there as well?

**Kids feel like they belong
when they know they are welcome.**

Think about what you do when you invite guests to your
home? You clean up. You organize the clutter. You sweep the
floor. You light a candle.

If they are staying overnight, you change the sheets, lay out
clean towels, and get food and drinks. It's simply your way of
letting someone know you were thinking about them *before*
they got there.

If you are expecting kids to show up at your church, you
should prepare the same way. You should create gathering
spaces that are welcoming.

**Kids feel like they belong
when they know it's for them.**

Occasionally, our staff needs to bring their young children into
work. So I keep a kids table with preschool toys in one of our
creative meeting spaces. The funny thing is, no one has to tell
the kids the table is for them. As soon as they see it, they walk
over, pull up a chair and sit down. They just know it's where
they belong.

One reason it's important to understand kids at different phases is so you can create unique spaces for them. What works for one phase of a kid's life will not necessarily work for another.

If you've walked through Pottery Barn Kids or Pottery Barn Teen, it's obvious someone in that organization understands different ages. They take a large, open storefront and create individual, age-specific environments. With the right paint color, posters, books, and props, they can make you feel like you have stepped right into the world of a fourth-grade boy.

You don't have to start with an attractive space or have Pottery Barn's marketing budget to be relevant. Even mobile or multipurpose environments can be transformed to make kids know they belong. And when you create age-specific spaces for kids and teenagers, your church sends a clear message that they are a priority.

It also sends a clear message to a parent: that their kid is welcome, that he or she is in a safe and inviting place, and that your church has been preparing for them before they walked through the door. But we will talk more about parents in the next chapter.

**Kids feel like they belong
when they know they are known.**

Your church will matter more to kids when they feel like it's a place where they are known. One of the most important things you can give any child or teenager is someone who knows…
how many fish are in their aquarium.
what they are doing next Saturday.
where they are going for vacation.
when they are going to have their birthday party.

In the book *Lead Small*, we explain five things a leader can do weekly to lead a child or a teenager. But your time is limited. You can only do those things for just *a few* kids. It's impossible to have the same kind of deep influence with a large group of kids that you can have when you are leading a few relationally.

That's why your church needs you to
do for a few kids what you wish you could do for every kid.

The truth is nothing in culture can compare to what consistent leaders and a caring community of faith can provide for a child or teenager. But that doesn't just happen. You have to become intentional about creating a safe, fun, caring place for kids to meet.

KIDS NEED A NEW KIND OF LEADER WHO WILL
IMPROVE THE ENVIRONMENT.

///

Someone, somewhere, had to build something,
book something, rent something, open something,
organize something, sweep something, light something, and
fix something so that your church could be a place where people
could belong. And if you want kids to know they belong, you
may have to update those things from time to time.

*What does your church look like for the people who actually
walk through the doors?*

Imagine walking into your church for the first time.
What does it smell like?
What does it look like?
What does it feel like?

*What would happen if you decided to take some personal
responsibility to improve your church in practical ways?*

Don't make the mistake of acting like it is only a pastor's job or
a committee's task to create the right kind of environments for
kids and teenagers.

How can your church have a reputation that's more inviting to your community?

Every time people drive or walk by the place where your church meets, they think about God. Or they at least may get some preconceived image of God in their mind. You have the potential to change how they see your church because you *are* the church. Even though your building may be the first impression people have of your church, you are the most important impression people have.

So how can you change the way your community sees your church? Here are a few thoughts (maybe you can pick one that sounds right for your community):

- ◯ Use more convicting words on your church sign.
- ◯ Offer unlimited donuts for every child.
- ◯ Guarantee sermons will only last 10 minutes.
- ◯ Hire a bear mascot to stand in the street and point one of those twirling signs at your church.
- ◯ Start making necessary improvements so every kid . . .

> feels more welcomed,
> stays more engaged,
> and firmly believes they have
> a place to belong in your church.

YOUR CHURCH MATTERS

BECAUSE IT'S A PLACE

WHAT IF YOU STARTED ACTING LIKE

YOU MAY BE THE BEST CHANCE A KID WILL HAVE TO FIND A PLACE TO BELONG

KIDS NEED
A NEW KIND
OF LEADER
WHO WILL

IMPROVE THE ENVIRONMENT

WHAT ARE SOME THINGS THAT WOULD MAKE YOUR
CHURCH'S ENVIRONMENTS FOR CHILDREN AND TEENAGERS
MORE WELCOMING, APPEALING, OR ENGAGING?

....

....

....

....

....

....

....

....

....

....

....

....

....

....

4

THERE'S A NEW KIND OF
LEADER WHO BELIEVES

EVERY FAMILY
MATTERS

REGARDLESS

THE CHURCH IS STRATEGICALLY POSITIONED IN CULTURE TO REMIND US THAT FAMILY MATTERS.

Most churches I know have family as a value. They talk about family from the platform, they celebrate family through their programming, and they hold on to a picture of what they think every family should look like. Even if it's unintentional, they seem to suggest that every family matters when it's
a married couple
with two or more biological children
who never fight about finances,
have weekly family devotions,
and teenagers who only listen to worship music.

The problem is that when I look around me,
there are a lot of families that don't look like that.

According to the most recent U.S. Census, only 20 percent of families in the United States are made up of married couples living with their own biological children. So what about all those other families?

What about the single parents, the adoptive parents, and the grandparents who live in our communities and carry the responsibility of raising kids? **If every family matters, then we may need to consider the possibility that every parent (or guardian) matters.**

Maybe we should amplify "every family."

Every person who is raising, nurturing, and parenting a kid or teenager matters. Regardless.

They matter regardless of their church attendance, denomination, nationality, political beliefs, marital status, gender, body piercings, education, weight, employment, citizenship, fashion preferences, PTA membership, tithing record, community service hours, or dental hygiene.

I know there's some controversy in that statement. That's okay. I'm not trying to take a political or theological stance on any of those issues. But before we can talk about how family matters, we need to at least agree that *every* family matters— even families that don't measure up to what some believe is the ideal standard for family.

Too often, churches are so focused on the picture of what they want families to become that they fail to build a bridge to where families actually are.

I'm not even sure the church can really lead families to see the bigger picture of God's love and restoration if we don't see it ourselves.

If we want to have influence on the faith of kids and teenagers, we need to change a few things about our view of their parents. Can we start by agreeing about three things?

Every parent matters because they matter to God.
Maybe that sounds too theological to be practical. But here's what it means: God created every parent in His image, and loves every parent enough to send His Son to die for them. If God cares that much about every parent, maybe we should too.

Every parent matters because they matter to their kid.
It's easy to notice what's broken about a family when you are on the outside looking in. But most kids care a great deal about their parents—regardless of their shortcomings. An MTV[1] survey found that 73 percent of kids said that their *parents* are the people who make them the happiest. So it's probably safe to assume that kids care how you treat their parents.

Every parent matters because their kids matter to them.
Even if they aren't disciplining their kids the way you would. Even if they don't feed their kids the kind of nutrition you might. Even if they haven't dressed their kids the way you wish. Every parent cares about the kids or teenagers in their home.

1 MTV/Associated Press Survey, "Youths' stuff of happiness may surprise parents," NBC News, August 20, 2007

What if you started acting like
**WHAT HAPPENS AT HOME IS MORE IMPORTANT
THAN WHAT HAPPENS AT CHURCH.**

Of course what happens at church is important, but what happens at home may be even more important.

The reason is simple—time.

When we started North Point Community Church, a few of us who worked with kids and teenagers realized something sobering. Even with the kids who attended our church consistently, at best we would only have about 40 hours with them every year. That's only 40 hours to help a kid understand everything they need to know about God, and the Bible, and life.

That same day, we calculated another number that shocked us: the amount of time the average parent gets to spend with their children. It was 3,000 hours in a single year.

When you simply consider the potential of 40 hours vs. 3,000 you can see why family matters.

No one has more potential to influence a kid than a parent.

That's because no one else will spend the same kind of time . . .
feeding,
cleaning,
transporting,
disciplining,
or loving that kid than their parent.

But here's something else that's true as well:
A parent isn't the only influence a kid needs.

Just like . . .
a pediatrician checks up on a kid's health,
a teacher advances a kid's education,
a coach develops a kid's fitness,
parents need other voices to remind them about what matters
when it comes to shaping their kid's faith.

But remember, nearly 75 percent of the people in your
community won't attend church this Sunday. And that
percentage includes a lot of parents.

The truth is, if parents don't think your church matters,
you will have a hard time influencing their family.

I'm not sure I know all the reasons that families outside the church don't go to church, but I think there are at least four.

1 Families outside the church don't TRUST us. Many parents feel as if church leaders have a motive. They assume we want to change them. They think we will turn their kid against them not toward them.

2 Families outside the church don't BELIEVE us. Many parents don't believe what church leaders say matters because we don't act like they matter. They don't believe that we really love them because we don't act like we even like them.

3 Families outside the church don't GET us. Many parents who don't go to church feel like the church is out-of touch with their issues. We just don't speak the same language. (When is the last time your waitress used the phrase "a hedge of protection"?)

4 Families outside the church don't NEED us. Parents look for help on Facebook before they look to the church. They have more resources than ever before and often see little real evidence that the church truly wants to help them win as parents.

Consider this.

Your church has one of two perspectives:

It's their problem. You can easily tell if this is your perspective. If it is, you probably sigh and shake your head a lot. The first thing you notice about a parent is usually something they aren't doing that they should be doing, or something that they should be doing that they aren't doing.

It's our mission. If you have this perspective, you are consumed with the question: What can I do to help?

If you want to change the way you see every family, then take the initiative to act like you really believe that *no one has more potential to influence a kid than a parent.* And make this simple decision: That it is your mission to help every parent win.

Maybe if we start making every family matter more to the church, the church will matter more to every family.

Or to say it another way: **We won't change the way families outside the church see us until we change the way we see them.**

There are two truths every leader should embrace if they want to make every family matter.

Every parent wants to be a good parent.
Maybe you're skeptical. That's okay. I've just never met a parent who walked out of the delivery room and said, "I can't wait to ruin this kid's life." Maybe they're out there. I just haven't met them.

Every parent can do something more.
That's true of the parent who volunteers at every church event and is fully engaged with your strategy, and it is also true of the parent who has never even heard of your church.

Can you imagine what would happen if all you did was help the average parent to do something more for their kid's faith than what they are currently doing?

What if . . .
a dad simply prayed with his son for the first time?
a grandma read a Bible story to her granddaughter?
a single mom got connected to a community of faith?

The church has unbelievable potential to influence a kid's faith when they believe in the potential of every parent to do something more.

KIDS NEED A NEW KIND OF LEADER WHO WILL
CONNECT WITH A PARENT.

///

If you want to be a new kind of leader, you will constantly look for ways to build a bridge to the family.

Practically speaking, you may need to . . .
introduce yourself.
give a parent your phone number.
send a text to let parents know what's going on.
show up where parents show up
(like at a middle school debate tournament).

You might have to do all of those things. And you might even have to do them more than once. Connection takes consistent effort. Imagine what would happen if you . . .
only talked to your boss through a monthly email.
only saw your best friend during the summer.
only called your mom on her birthday.

Just remember, there is nothing in culture that can compare to what you can do for a family if you show up consistently to care about a kid's faith and future.

I recently spoke at a church to a group of parents about the importance of family. When I finished the message, a mom, holding her two-year-old-daughter, came up to me. She was a single parent, living in her parents' house. She looked right at me and said, "I just want to know if my daughter is going to be okay." Her picture of family hadn't worked out the way she had planned. She told me how alone she felt. She wanted to know she could find some other people who would help her fight for her daughter's future.

Every parent needs . . .
to have an ally, so they don't feel alone.
to know what to do today, so they have a plan.
to see how they are winning, so they have hope.

This week, you have the potential to influence a parent simply by reminding them of the important work they're doing. When you show up consistently for their son or daughter, you have an opportunity to tell a parent something positive about their son or daughter that they might have forgotten. When you look for ways a parent is doing something right, you can encourage them to keep at it.

EVERY FAMILY MATTERS

REGARDLESS

WHAT IF YOU STARTED ACTING LIKE

WHAT HAPPENS AT HOME IS MORE IMPORTANT THAN WHAT HAPPENS AT CHURCH

KIDS NEED
A NEW KIND
OF LEADER
WHO WILL

**CONNECT WITH
A PARENT**

MAKE A LIST OF SOME FAMILIES YOU KNOW INSIDE AND
OUTSIDE OF YOUR CHURCH.

....

....

....

....

....

....

....

....

....

....

....

....

....

WRITE DOWN SOME WAYS YOU COULD ENCOURAGE AND
SERVE THOSE FAMILIES.

....

....

....

....

....

....

....

....

....

....

....

....

....

5

THERE'S A NEW KIND OF
LEADER WHO BELIEVES

THE TRUTH
MATTERS

WHEN LOVE MATTERS

GIRLS WHO ARE THREE AND THIRTEEN YEARS OLD
HAVE AT LEAST ONE THING IN COMMON.

They are hard to argue with about anything.

It doesn't matter how logical, reasonable,
or convincing your argument is,
you probably won't win.

And it doesn't matter who else agrees with your point of view.
You can have the Bible, The Library of Congress, Dr. Phil, and
Billy Graham all on your side.

You are still wrong.

Why?
Because in a preschool or middle school girl's mind,
it doesn't matter if you are right.
It doesn't even matter if it's true.

It really only matters if it matters.
Actually, it really only matters if it matters to them.

Does that mean truth doesn't matter?
No. Truth always matters.

Here are a few things to consider about truth:

THE BIBLE IS TRUE.
We don't have time for an intense and analytical debate on
the authority and accuracy of Scripture. But I'll just assume
that you believe, "All Scripture is given by the inspiration of
God, and is profitable . . ."

*That's why the Bible should be the primary source for what you
are teaching kids.*

EVERY TRUTH IS NOT IN THE BIBLE.
Okay. Before you think I'm a heretic, just imagine some of the
things you need to say to a preschooler or middle schooler
that are not in the Bible. You can decide which ones go with
each age group.

"It's called underwear because it goes under."
"Going swimming is not the same as taking a bath."
"Private parts are meant to be private."
"Anything you text or post will be there forever."
"It's deodorant and you put it on every day."
"Just because you *can* eat it, doesn't mean you *should*."

*That's why, if you want to help kids, you may need to know
some things that are not in the Bible.*

EVERY TRUTH DOES NOT MATTER EQUALLY.
Some truths in the Bible are more important than others. It's not because they are more true. It's just because they are more significant as it relates to what matters in life. Even Jesus implied that one commandment was the "greatest".

That just means someone has to prioritize which truths are most critical for kids to learn.

EVERY TRUTH DOES NOT MATTER TO EVERYONE.
That's why we talk about phases so much. The truths that are most applicable in your life may not be the most applicable for a middle schooler. While you might not teach the story of David and Bathsheba to your preschoolers, you might do a month-long study on the life of David with your high schoolers. Some truths are more meaningful and applicable at one phase than they are at another.

That's why you need to understand some unique things about how kids learn and think at every phase.

Truth always matters, but when it comes to people of all sizes and ages, truth matters more when it actually matters to them.

So your job as leader is to take
a truth that matters and . . .
reword it,
reframe it,
repackage it,
reimagine it,
until it matters to a child or teenager.

Another word for this idea is *relevance*.

A lot of leaders get confused by that term. They think
relevance means "contemporary" or "trendy." The problem is
what you say can actually be current, creative, engaging, and
true and still not be relevant.

Relevance simply means
"connecting to the matter at hand."

When you are relevant, you connect *what is true* to *what is real*
in a kid's world. What you say on Sunday should make sense
for a teenager on Monday. That's why you need to know more
about what happens in their world on Monday.

When you are relevant, you don't compromise the integrity
of a truth, you elevate the value of a truth. Irrelevance, on the
other hand, paralyzes truth.

What if you started acting like
**YOU NEED TO UNDERSTAND A KID'S WORLD IF
YOU WANT TO HAVE INFLUENCE IN A KID'S LIFE.**

It's an interesting tension.
Sometimes you think the better you know the truth, the better
you can influence kids with the truth. But we want to reverse
that for a moment. We want you to consider the idea that the
better you know kids, the better you can influence them with
the truth.

What if the best way to make truth matter more in the life
of a teenager is to make sure the teenager matters more in
your life?

That doesn't mean you need go back to college and major in
elementary or secondary education. But when you understand
more about child development, it will actually help you teach
the Bible.

Be careful. You can be so passionate in your zeal to be
theologically correct that you miss connecting with the hearts
of people. The Pharisees missed it, some Christians in the
early church missed it, and it's easy to miss it with kids.

When Andy Stanley, pastor of North Point Community Church, talks about teaching, he explains that "we don't begin with theology, but we begin with what we have in common—fears, joys, challenges, and a need for love—and that draws people in . . .""

That's why we often tell leaders who work with kids that there's a difference in teaching the Bible to kids, and teaching kids the Bible.

Both phrases sound the same. But take a closer look. The second statement starts with *kids*. It's our way of saying you need to . . .
know,
understand,
and love
the child before you should expect to teach the child anything that will have a lasting impact.

Most children and teenagers will remember how you made them *feel* far longer than they will remember what you said. That's why . . .
The truth matters when love matters.
What you say will matter more to kids when they know they matter to you.

No wonder Paul wrote to "speak the truth in love."

The truths that matter most in a child or teenager's life should
be taught in the context of a loving relationship, not just in
a classroom. Kids will learn concepts like grace, forgiveness,
patience, service, and peace through interaction with leaders
who actually model the character of God.

I would amplify the principle this way:
You can't speak the truth in love
if you don't love who you are speaking to.

That statement probably bothers some of you. You know why?
Because it ends with the word "to." And it freaks you out a
little when someone ends a sentence with a preposition. It's
just wrong grammar. And right now, you care more about
fixing it than you do thinking about what it means. That's kind
of the point.

It's just easier to . . .
correct what's wrong than to cultivate what's right.
stand for something than to love someone.
fight for a truth than to fight for the heart.
craft a message than to get messy.

As important as any truth is, you need to decide that love comes first. That's why, if you want kids to embrace certain truths for their lifetime, you may have to go deeper in their lives than you had planned.

Lasting change happens in someone's heart when we lead with friendship and compassion.

I have always been inspired by how church leaders in the city engage in the holistic issues related to a child. Many of these leaders actively collaborate with other influencers to forge solutions for the social, health, and economic challenges that families face in their communities.

I love what my friend Virginia Ward says,
"The churches in my community have to address the education and economic concerns that are paralyzing children. If they don't address the systemic issues families are facing, then it just doesn't make sense to only talk about Jesus."

I'm going to make a suggestion. Leaders in the church are not losing influence in their communities because they are not teaching the truth. They are losing influence because they are not teaching with love.

You primarily have influence with a child or teenager in one of the following ways:
Power—you are physically stronger.
Authority—you are in charge.
Love—you have a relationship.

The first two are temporary. But a smart leader understands the potential of the third one to make a lasting impact.

Take your cue from Jesus.

If anyone could have leveraged his power,
Jesus could have,
since He is all-powerful.

If anyone could have leveraged his authority,
Jesus could have,
since He has all authority.

But He didn't. Instead Jesus became like you and like me, so He could have a different kind of influence—*that's empathy.*

Jesus stepped into our shoes, so He could show up and authenticate truth in a different kind of way.

KIDS NEED A NEW KIND OF LEADER WHO WILL
THINK LIKE SOMEONE ELSE.

We define empathy as *the ability to press pause on your own thoughts and feelings long enough to explore someone else's thoughts and feelings.*

If you don't pause long enough to think like someone else you will . . .
make assumptions that you shouldn't make.
think you know what you don't really know.
miss the opportunities you have to connect.

It may be that we have forgotten the importance of empathy. Or it may be that it's difficult sometimes to have empathy for a kid.

Empathy is about connecting and understanding,
but honestly, some things are just hard to understand, like . . .
why it's infuriating when someone wipes your nose.
why a pile of firewood is laugh-until-you-cry funny.

So before you teach a kid truth,
you may need to take a walk in their world
(in your imagination or in reality).

That's another way of saying, you need to . . .
see what they see.
read what they read.
hear what they hear.
feel what they feel.
know what they know.

The problem is that it's hard to think like someone else. When it comes to thinking like kids at every phase, it's especially challenging to remember what we need to remember due to the fact that . . .

It's *impossible* to remember what it was like in preschool—nobody does.

It's *difficult* to remember what it was like in elementary school—it was a long time ago.

It's *scary* to remember what it was like in middle school—most of us have blocked it from our memories.

It's *easy* to remember what it was like in high school—but remember that's what it was like for you in 1985, and is not what it's like for students today.

If you are going to lead with empathy, you need to do one of two things in a kid's world: Imagine or interact.

When you IMAGINE a kid's world, you . . .
pause to consider how they are feeling.
pause to learn what they are experiencing.
pause before you assume their motive.
pause to anticipate what they are thinking.

When you INTERACT with a kid, you . . .
pause to play a game.
pause to listen to a joke.
pause to eat a meal.
pause to watch a talent show.

You get the idea. If you want to lead kids with empathy, you have to make an intentional investment of time and energy.

Loving a child or teenager will require that you do something and go somewhere. If you want kids to show up at your church to learn truth, you will need to show up in their world and learn about them. If you want the truth to matter, then make love matter more.

THE TRUTH
MATTERS

WHEN LOVE MATTERS

WHAT IF YOU STARTED ACTING LIKE

YOU NEED TO UNDERSTAND A KID'S WORLD IF YOU WANT TO HAVE INFLUENCE IN A KID'S LIFE

KIDS NEED
A NEW KIND
OF LEADER
WHO WILL

**THINK LIKE
SOMEONE ELSE**

WRITE DOWN THE NAMES OF THE KIDS OR TEENAGERS YOU
ARE INFLUENCING.

....

....

....

....

....

....

....

....

....

....

....

....

....

MAKE A LIST OF NEW THINGS YOU'RE LEARNING ABOUT
THEM AND UPDATE IT CONTINUALLY.

6

THERE'S A NEW KIND OF
LEADER WHO BELIEVES

DOING GOOD
MATTERS

IF YOU'RE HUMAN

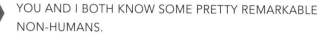

YOU AND I BOTH KNOW SOME PRETTY REMARKABLE
NON-HUMANS.
ROBOCOP
HAL 9000
R2-D2
BAYMAX

But even in the best stories, like ones where the robot aids the destruction of the Death Star, the robot is never fully the same as its human companion.

Maybe they are programmed to recognize evil. Maybe they have enough rationality to win at chess. Maybe they learn how to imitate social behaviors like a fist bump. But a robot doesn't feel the kind of empathy we talked about in the last chapter. A robot doesn't imagine. And a robot doesn't show compassion. That's distinctly human.

There's actually nothing in all of creation that has the same capacity to care,
empathize,
or imagine like a human.
(Who do you think programmed all those robots?)

I believe humans have a unique capacity for one reason. They were made in the image of God.

In case you haven't noticed, *kids are human too.*

Stop for a moment and think about it. If every kid is created in the image of God, then every kid has a divine capacity . . .
to believe, imagine, and love.
to care, relate, and trust.
to reason, improve, and lead.
That's a lot of potential.

Some of us have been so programmed to see what's wrong with kids and teenagers, we have forgotten to see what's right about them.

It's easy to think that because they aren't . . .
old enough,
smart enough,
mature enough,
important enough,
or even spiritual enough,
they can't really do anything significant.

I actually think it's ironic that some non-Christian organizations understand the potential of a kid better than many churches. Just look at Disney.

Not only do kids have a divine *capacity* to do good, kids were made to do good.

See if this makes sense:
If God is good
and God made people in His image,
then people were made to do good
. . . *and that includes kids and teenagers.*

For over 10 years, Orange has been championing the potential of kids and teenagers, which means we hear a lot of remarkable stories about what kids and teenagers are doing in our country and around the world. When I hear about some of the good things that kids and teenagers are capable of doing, I am actually reminded of how good God is.

When you remember that every kid is made in the image of God, it can change . . .
how you see them.
how you see God.

When you remember that every kid is made in the image of God, and you give them opportunities to do good, it can change . . .
how they see themselves.
how they see God.

What if you started acting like

WHAT A KID DOES CAN ACTUALLY AFFECT WHAT A KID BELIEVES.

Okay. This might sound backwards, so let me clarify. A person's beliefs obviously influence their behavior. We seem to talk about that a lot.

But I sometimes wonder if we have forgotten that, practically speaking, our behaviors can also influence our beliefs. I actually think the things a person does sometimes have a transformative impact on what they believe.

Think about this for a minute. Let's say you're going to teach a class on mountain climbing. You talk about climbing, show pictures from climbing, maybe even pass around some climbing equipment. If you did all of these things, but the students in your class never experienced climbing for themselves, how motivated do you think they would be to go climbing?

Here is a profound question: Do you think climbers climb just because they have heard about climbing, or because one day they started climbing? Experience can have a profound impact.

When we started North Point Community Church, we decided we were not going to create programming for teenagers on Sunday mornings. We didn't want them to go to a class where they would sit and have a Bible study. Instead, we decided we would give them opportunities to serve with us on Sunday mornings. We wanted teenagers to serve not just because we needed their help, but because we instinctively knew it would be essential for their spiritual growth.

Consider how this has worked in your own life. Was there a time when you plugged in and served? What did that do for your faith? If I had to guess, I would imagine that it affected what you believe about people, about yourself, and maybe even about God. If that's true for you, why wouldn't it be true for teenagers as well?

One of the best ways to stimulate faith is to give someone an opportunity to have a personal ministry.

It's kind of like that mountain climbing illustration.
If you never actually climb . . .
you will miss the wonder of seeing the view.
you will miss the discovery of personal capacity.
you will miss the passion of engaging with the mountain.

If you want a kid's faith to grow significantly, give them something significant to do.

It's important to understand how what a kid does relates to what they believe as a Christian.

Doing good is a response to the Gospel.
It's not a substitute for the Gospel.
A kid's ability to do good can be a reminder of what Jesus has already done. It reinforces the power of the Gospel to work in your daily life.

Doing good reflects the nature of Jesus.
It doesn't earn you points with God.
God's love is unconditional and your salvation is a result of His grace. When a kid reflects on the nature of Christ, it is a reminder to them that He doesn't measure their behavior and that He loves them unconditionally.

Doing good stretches your faith.
It's not a replacement for faith.
There is a subtle difference between putting your faith in what you can do and what God can do through you. But when kids and teenagers experience the difference, they will continue to mature in what God designed them to do.

In fact, I think you should probably be cautious about any theology that says you shouldn't help kids do good things. Why? For a lot of reasons. But here's at least one.

Sometimes kids will understand a little more about God when they do something God made them to do.

That can actually be true for non-Christian kids as well.

Doing good sparks the image of God in every kid.
When you help a kid discover what they were made to do, you have an opportunity to introduce them to the God who made them.

Doing good connects every kid to a bigger story.
Serving others turns one's mind and heart outward. It reminds us that this life is bigger than just our story. And when a kid begins to see a bigger story at work, you have an opportunity to talk about the One who is redeeming the story.

So, what if your job as a leader is simply to . . .
appeal to the nature of Christ in every kid who believes.
appeal to the image of God in every kid who was created to know Him.

KIDS NEED A NEW KIND OF LEADER WHO WILL
ENLIST TEENAGERS TO SERVE.

I know what you're thinking, "Wait, teenagers? Why just teenagers? Shouldn't every kid serve at every phase?"

Sure. Go ahead. Try that.
Have your toddlers organize the food pantry.
Ask your kindergartners to fund a missionary family.
Enlist your second graders to raise awareness for sex trafficking.

Okay. Maybe those aren't the best ideas—unless of course, you have a Plan B for funding that missionary family.

But you're right. Every kid at every phase should experience what God can do through their life. So maybe you should consider how to . . .
prompt preschoolers to share.
rotate elementary kids to help each other.
invite middle schoolers to serve alongside adults.
enlist high schoolers to develop a weekly personal ministry.

The truth is this: The more we learn about different phases, the more we are convinced that serving becomes a bigger deal as a kid gets older.

Brain research actually gives some interesting insight into teenagers. Researcher Ronald E. Dahl put it this way: "Adolescence is a developmental period when an appetite for adventure, a predilection for risk, and a desire for novelty and thrills seem to reach naturally high levels."[1]

In other words, teenagers are experience magnets.

One of the reasons some students struggle to connect with church is because we invite them to something that is static and uneventful. They never experience the intoxicating kind of faith that comes when they allow God to work through their lives. They don't have a hands-on encounter with ministry that gives them a personal sense of God's mission. They miss out on the passion that results from colliding with humanity when caring for someone in a crisis situation.

Teenagers are especially drawn to anywhere they can find adventure and significance. So, if you want to engage a teenager, give them somewhere to serve.

1 Adolescent Brain Development: A Period of Vulnerabilities and Opportunities Keynote Address Ronald E. Dahl Psychiatry and Pediatrics, University of Pittsburgh Medical Center, Pittsburgh, Pennsylvania 15213, USA pg. 7- 8

Here's another reason to focus on teenagers: Enlisting teenagers to serve will change everyone.

Kids need to experience teenagers serving.
Have you ever observed a second grader as they watch an eighth grader? Teenagers have a lot of influence. Enlisting teenagers to serve can change a lot of kids.

Teenagers need to serve alongside adults.
Even though they might not show it, teenagers are learning how to become adults *from* adults. And what they see adults do will influence them more than what they hear adults say.

Adults need to see teenagers serving.
When adults see teenagers serving, both inside and outside the church, it changes how they see teenagers.

So the question is: *How will you enlist teenagers to serve?* What is your role in inviting someone to experience doing good—not so they will put their trust in good, but so they will put their trust in God? That's when they will see how God wants to work through their life. And that's when they will begin to say, "I was made for this!"

DOING GOOD MATTERS

IF YOU'RE HUMAN

WHAT IF YOU STARTED ACTING LIKE

WHAT A KID DOES CAN ACTUALLY AFFECT WHAT A KID BELIEVES

KIDS NEED
A NEW KIND
OF LEADER
WHO WILL

ENLIST A
TEENAGER
TO SERVE

WHAT TEENAGERS DO YOU PERSONALLY KNOW BOTH INSIDE
AND OUTSIDE THE CHURCH? WRITE DOWN A FEW IDEAS FOR
HOW THEY COULD SERVE OTHERS AND MEET A NEED.

IF YOU ARE A TEENAGER, CONSIDER THE NEEDS THAT YOU
SEE IN YOUR CHURCH OR COMMUNITY. WRITE DOWN A FEW
IDEAS FOR HOW YOU CAN HELP.

7

THERE'S A NEW KIND OF
LEADER WHO BELIEVES

THIS WEEK
MATTERS

WHEN IT'S REPEATED

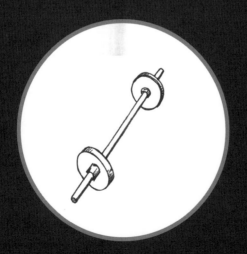

THERE ARE APPROXIMATELY 936 WEEKS FROM THE TIME A BABY IS BORN UNTIL THEY GROW UP AND MOVE OUT.

Sometimes when I speak to parents, I challenge them to get a jar and fill it with 936 marbles. Then I ask them to reduce the number of marbles in the jar to the actual number of weeks their child has left at home before graduation. Their next assignment is to keep removing one marble each week.

There's nothing special about a jar of marbles. But something happens when a parent begins to quantify the amount of time they have left with a kid. The jar is a constant visual reminder of something that's absolutely essential if you want to influence a kid or teenager: TIME.

936 weeks may seem like a lot,
but it goes by fast.

Just think about the number of weeks a leader actually has to influence a kid's faith.

A first grader has 624 weeks.
A sixth grader has 364 weeks.
A ninth grader has 209 weeks.
A senior has 52 weeks . . . and counting.

**This week matters
when you make it count.**

Putting a visual number to the time you have left isn't a new idea. One wise leader said it this way:

"Teach us to number our days, that we may gain a heart of wisdom." (Psalm 90:12)

So, how does counting your days (or weeks)
give you a heart of wisdom?
I'm not sure.
But I can guess.

Think about what happens with the countdown clock in a basketball game. As the clock gets closer to zero, the intensity increases. The players become more focused.

In the same way, visualizing the weeks you have left to influence a kid may help you . . .
pace yourself,
narrow your focus,
guard your margin,
value quality interaction,
and become more intentional about what you do.

**This week matters
when you add it to next week and the next . . .**

The jar of marbles is also a reminder of the potential you
have when you consider how you invest in a kid over multiple
weeks. What you do this week matters, but you can't get it all
done this week. That's why it takes a collection of weeks to
influence a kid.

It's kind of like exercise. I don't usually use sports analogies (I
assume you have to know a lot about sports to pull that off).
But whenever I see an ad for something that makes you lose
weight instantly or build muscle overnight, I usually assume it's
a scam.

Some things take time.
Some things take repetition.

Some things can't be accomplished in one week.
It takes multiple weeks to . . .
discover a vaccine.
write a novel.
learn how to play the violin.
grow a hipster beard.
influence a child.

If you want to influence a kid's future, you have to resist the temptation to take shortcuts. There is no such thing as instant faith or character.

**This week matters
even when you don't think it matters.**

Did you every stop to consider:
The reason you can't see spiritual growth
is because it's too spiritual?
The reason you can't predict significant moments
is because they are unpredictable?

When you lead kids and teenagers, there may be weeks when you get discouraged. Let's be honest. Most of the time, you will never hear . . .
a baby say, "Thank you for changing my diaper."
a toddler say, "I'm so grateful that you spent Friday night sorting craft supplies for our activity."
a teenager say, "Wow, that talk you gave really changed my perspective."

But maybe the best thing you can do is to choose to keep . . .
investing in what you can't see.
being present for what is not happening.
trusting that time will do what God designed it to do.

What if you started acting like
**WHAT YOU DO THIS WEEK MATTERS MORE
WHEN YOU DO IT EVERY WEEK.**

I could make the argument that God had an "every week" approach. Maybe He actually created time so He could communicate something that could only be communicated through multiple weeks?

Why didn't God send Jesus as soon as Adam and Eve ate the fruit? He could have resolved the issue then and there. But He waited. He used centuries of weeks to keep His promises and build relationships.

He gave Abraham a son.
He let Joseph sit in jail.
He sent Moses to deliver a people.
He let a nation wander in the desert for decades.

It was as if God decided,
"I can help you understand something with time that you could never really understand in a moment."

If God proved His love for us week after week over time, then maybe that's the best way to cultivate what matters in the hearts of kids and teenagers.

The most significant gifts we can give the next generation are what we give them over time. That makes what you do this week, and next week, and the week after, strategic.

What you do every week will matter more in someone's life when you do it . . .
week after week,
month after month,
year after year.

Jimmy Mellado knows the power of what happens week after week in a kid's life. After 20 years leading Willow Creek Association to help churches win every week, Jimmy became president of Compassion International to help kids win every week.

Jimmy is a strategist and a thought leader. Whenever I'm around him, I can't take notes fast enough. He has an MBA from Harvard and was an Olympic decathlete. And when he talks about kids, he gets emotional. Sometimes we both cry, which can be a little awkward in public.

Mellado is convinced that if you can connect a church to the same kids week after week it radically changes their future. And he has research to prove it.

Compassion had a turning point in the 1980s when they started working solely through local churches.

Economist Bruce Wydick conducted a study of more than 10,000 grown Compassion children to show the organization's approach nearly doubled the chances of kids completing secondary school and increased college graduation rates by 40 to 80 percent.

Again, what distinguishes Compassion International from other groups is that Compassion only sponsors children through churches.

As a result, those churches provide 4,000 hours of contact with a loving caregiver during the most at-risk years of a sponsored child's life. Meanwhile, other organizations, usually using social workers, only have 40 contact hours. This astounding 4,000 vs. 40-hour difference means Compassion has a direct, intentional impact in the life of every kid every week.

It's ironic. While this book is trying to make sure every church in America still has kids, Compassion's goal is to make sure every child around the world has a church. They understand the value a consistent leader brings to a kid's life week after week. We could learn a lot from their approach.

KIDS NEED A NEW KIND OF LEADER WHO WILL
KEEP SHOWING UP.

//

Just like the people in ancient times developed their view of God as . . .
the God of Abraham,
the God of Isaac,
or the God of Moses,

You have developed a sense of who God is because you have met . . .
the God of Susan,
the God of Carlos,
or the God of Jeff.

God uses people. That's the point. He always has. Sometimes we forget that the God of the Bible is the God of the people of the Bible. God has always used people to demonstrate His story of redemption.

Please don't miss this.
Kids can't see God.
Kids can't see Jesus.
Kids can't see the Holy Spirit.

But kids can see people who follow God.

Kids can see you.

The best chance someone may have to personally see God is to get a close-up look at the people who follow Him. That's why your mission is simple: Show up in a kid's life so they can see God.

Okay. Maybe you're thinking,

"Doesn't it take a little more than just showing up?"

"What do I do once I get there?"

Here's an answer to help you get started. You show up to help a kid do at least four things:

1. **Hear** from God by navigating the Bible, listening to stories of faith, and personalizing Scripture.
2. **Pray** to God together and learn to pray personally and privately for the needs of others.
3. **Talk** about God with friends and other adults who trust Him.
4. **Live** for God through giving, service, praise, and obedience.

When you show up week after week to help a kid hear, pray, talk, and live for God, you solidify faith skills that will outlast your personal influence. Just remember, showing up this week matters more *when you do it every week*.

Preschoolers need someone to show up weekly so they see a familiar face. Just think about what happens when you put a two-year-old on Santa's lap. Preschoolers may be afraid of even the kindest, most generous adult if the leader only shows up once a year.

Elementary kids need someone to show up weekly so they know you know them. Kids are eager to feel seen and known by adults. They need someone who knows their name, their interests, and their pet's name.

Middle schoolers need someone to show up weekly so they know you know them NOW. Things have changed since last week—they may have changed since last night. So, it's probably good to show up more than once a week. There's a lot to keep up with.

High schoolers need someone to show up weekly so they know you will be there when they need you.
Eventually they will hit a wall, make a bad decision, or feel defeated—and it might not always happen on a Sunday. So when it happens, they need to know who to turn to.

A new kind of leader will keep showing up weekly because they know it's the best way for a kid to experience a consistent relationship with God.

THIS WEEK MATTERS

WHEN IT'S REPEATED

WHAT IF YOU STARTED ACTING LIKE

WHAT YOU DO THIS WEEK MATTERS MORE WHEN YOU DO IT EVERY WEEK

KIDS NEED
A NEW KIND
OF LEADER
WHO WILL

**KEEP
SHOWING
UP**

WRITE DOWN SOME WAYS YOU CAN ENCOURAGE A KID
OR TEENAGER TO HEAR, PRAY, TALK, AND LIVE FOR GOD
THIS WEEK AND EVERY WEEK. (IF YOU WANT A FEW PHASE-
SPECIFIC IDEAS, YOU CAN DOWNLOAD A FREE TIMELINE
FROM WWW.JUSTAPHASE.COM.)

....

....

....

....

....

....

....

....

....

....

....

....

....

....

....

....

....

....

....

....

....

....

....

....

....

....

....

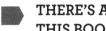

THERE'S A LOT
THIS BOOK DIDN'T SAY.

I didn't explain how . . .
a pastor named Kirk inspired the idea.
half of this book was written at Bantam & Biddy.
there are another six beliefs that didn't make the cut.
I wish we could write another book on chapter five.
I was inspired to buy many antique doors.

If I had been writing a book on theology, the subjects would
have included . . .
the Gospel Matters.
your Faith Matters.
God's Grace Matters.
Jesus Matters.

Anyone who really knows us is very aware that those values are
deep in our DNA as an organization. They drive everything we
create and produce.

But a lead pastor of a church without any staff asked me, "Do
you have a resource I can give my volunteers and leaders that
explains how and why we should make children a priority?"
And then he said, "And it really can't take very long to read."

So I decided to be practical.

It's simple really.

We believe that Jesus stands at the door of everyone's life
to say,

*"Here I am! I stand at the door and knock. If anyone hears
my voice and opens the door, I will come in and eat with that
person, and they with me."*

Anyone who has opened that door knows that following Jesus
changes everything.

He didn't knock and say, "Let me come in so I can tell you
something." Or "Let me come in so I can explain what you are
doing wrong."

He simply said, "I want to come in and eat with you, and then
you can eat with me."

Jesus is just that way. He gently knocks and when we say,
"yes", He immediately becomes an amazing host who
welcomes us into a new way of living.

When someone invites Jesus into their life, Jesus invites them
to experience a life of opening doors.

This book was written to ask you to be a new kind of leader because there is generation of children and teenagers who need to be connected to people who know what it's like to follow Jesus. And it only makes sense that if you have opened the door to Jesus then you have the potential to help a kid do the same. So keep opening doors.

Open a door to *whoever* He loves.
There are some kids and teenagers in your circle of influence that need to experience God's unconditional love. You may be their best chance to understand how much God really loves them.

Open a door to *whatever* He can do.
For the record, most leaders never feel qualified to lead kids. The good news is it's never only about what you can do. When you consider what God can do, anything is possible.

Open a door to *wherever* He takes you.
This is an unpredictable journey. There are no promises that things will always work out the way you pictured. It will be hard to tell if what you are doing is really working. But even when things don't go according to your plan, I can guarantee you that it will be worth it.

By the way, you may even have to knock on a few doors and step into a few places where you feel uncomfortable. When you get involved in kids or teenagers lives, it can get messy. Just remember, it's not your job to change them, it's your responsibility to love them.

I know what you may be thinking,
"If someone lets me into their life,
what should I say? How should I act?"

Don't worry. It's only dinner.
Just show up and be present.
I suspect you will know what to do when the time comes.

IF YOU BELIEVE DO SOMETHING

KIDS MATTER		**VOLUNTEER TO DO SOMETHING MORE**
A STRATEGY MATTERS		**PLAY AS A TEAM**
YOUR CHURCH MATTERS		**IMPROVE THE ENVIRONMENT**
EVERY FAMILY MATTERS		**CONNECT WITH A PARENT**
THE TRUTH MATTERS		**THINK LIKE SOMEONE ELSE**
DOING GOOD MATTERS		**ENLIST A TEENAGER TO SERVE**
WHAT YOU DO THIS WEEK MATTERS		**KEEP SHOWING UP**